A Penny for Your Thoughts

Penny Johnson's Legacy

PENNY JOHNSON

A
Penny
for
Your
Thoughts

A Penny for Your Thoughts

PENNY JOHNSON

ARPress
ILLUMINATING IDEAS
EMPOWERING VOICES

ARPress
45 Dan Road Suite 5
Canton MA 02021

Hotline: 1(800) 220-7660
Fax: 1(855) 752-6001

Ordering Information:
Quantity sales. Special discounts are available on quantity purchases by corporations, associations, and others. For details, contact the publisher at the address above.

Printed in the United States of America.

ISBN-13:   Paperback   979-8-89676-006-1
              eBook   979-8-89676-007-8

Library of Congress Control Number: 2024925144

Dedicated to my Grandparents

Anna Mariah and Robert Potter Coldiron
    (Mimie)   (Daddy Bob)
Who raised me in respect and love

In appreciation to Robert Nelson who
first published my Poetry Nationally
In American Poetry Anthology

Heartfelt Thanks to my husband who
never left my side as I wrote this
book, a real labor of love

About the Book

"A Penny for Your Thoughts" is a poetry book to delight, inform, insprire, uplift, entertain, surprise and spiritually enhance any lover of poetry

Penny believes poetry is a gift the poet gives as he or she has received and that poetry is the song the poet sings to beautify the whole world

Her inspiration comes from her favorite Poet, Walt Whitman

A Poem for Peace

We can't have peace, we don't
believe we can
Until every person belongs to
the family of man
We must say to humanity today
that peace is the only way

Who are we? We are you and I
We can't have peace if we don't
try
We must care about each other every
where in every way,
Then peace would be just a breath away
Riding on transparent wings here to
stay!
World peace will begin when there is
peace within, each of us

The Purpose of a Poet

When a poet writes about under
standing, happiness and joy
It is an art because it comes
from the poet's heart
But
When a poet writes about love
it comes straight down from
God up above
Listen now, if you don't
already know it
God speaks softly through
the poet

My Husband, My Sons

Willie
We are what we constantly do
You always do what you say you'll do
That's exactly why that I love you
Buddy
What did you say, It made my heart
swell
You said "Anything worth doing is
worth doing well"
Do I have a son? Yes! A wonderful
one
Robbie
Since first I bounced you on my knee
I knew exactly what you'd be
Anything and everything the world
allowed
You were born to make me proud!

I Will

Death does not win, Dennis
My baby boy, my pride and joy
In your brief life, only one day
Tiny precious one, may I say
Gladly I carried you beneath my heart
for nine months, proudly I will carry
you in my heart forever
I Will!

A Jewel

A red-haired beauty, my grand-daughter
is so loving and sweet
She's someone you would surely love to meet
So full of life, each day she sings with joy
I'm so glad she wasn't born a boy
For she sparkles and does she shine
I'm so glad that she is mine
A jewel is what she is
Priceless like a pearl
Yes, a pearl
My little girl

Penny Johnson

Our Gentle Giant

At sixteen "shine" like a diamond up in the sky
Live life to its fullest
Here's the reason why

Huge in stature, a tackle on the football team
A large and "growly bear" to others you may seem

You're sensitive blue eyes say otherwise
For you are sensitive, creative, musical and kind
A more loving grand-son no one could ever find
Big tall and strong you know right from wrong
With your sense of humor and heart of pure gold
Young man, you are going places
When all is said and told "Shine on!"

Awesome

Silence
Stillness
Coolness
SUDDENLY
Quickly
quickly
gently
falling
falling
rising
rising
glistening
shimmering
beautiful
Snow

IRON WILL

The mighty windstorm forces the weeping
willow tree's branches down, down almost
into the ground

Leaves and trunk "groan" and twril side
to side, up and down
A horrible sight! What a fright!

Sprawling and deep roots hold the tree
tight and upright, steadfast till the
last

Wild winds may make the weeping willow
tree sway and shake
           But,
The weeping willow tree may bend but
it will not break

A Mighty Leader

Does a leader step out front and others
fall in behind
        Or,
Does a leader line up last, pushing others
forward to reach their goal line

Are leaders born or are they made
Do they "rise up" from long hard work
        Or
Do they "think and plan" resting in the
shade

Can people make it without a leader anyway?
Or must a leader lead every single day

If you are a leader, you know it Don't tell others how to live
Show it!

For a leader's gift is to bring others up
        so,
They can drink from life's victory cup!

Satire

Be The Star You Are

Hollywood is home to stars they say
Be beautiful and blond, handsome is the way
Take acting lessons, diction and tone
Be dumb as a rock but don't let it be known
Change your name from Fitzgerald Johnathan
McDuff to a more macho, western sound like
"Stone Bluff"
The fans look up to you, you're their fantasy
Your whole life is a lie but protect it so
no one can ever see
Be a lover, married 5 times and have a
divorce or two
Have lots of children, fight their fathers
for them
It's the Hollywood thing to do
Have a face lift, tummy tuck, color your hair
Man or woman anything is fair
Forget your parents wanted you to be a Doctor or lawyer,
When they saw you in Hollywood their hearts sank
Forget about them think only of yourself and
cry all the way to the bank

Beauty Beyond Belief

Leaves of a scarlet, gold and purple hue
Swaying on tree limbs, "Falls" way of uplifting
you
By day a brisk breeze, night falls, almost a
freeze
Each day more gorgeous than the one before
Moving forward, more beauty much more

Bits of ice crystals on windows of cars
Heads turn upward to drink in the stars
Harvest is coming soon
Look at the moon

October takes our breath away
Soon November is here to stay
But October's memory will never go away!

Fright Night

"Frost on the pumpkin" and on the ground
Spooky little goblins running all around
Dark zombies, witches, blood sucking bats
Gorillas, vampires and lots of black cats

Clowns, ghosts, angels with wings
Cinderella, Snow White, ballerinas
Beautiful, fanciful, as well as "scary" things
"Strange" visitors at our front door

Get the candy, here comes a lot more
Don't faint, don't worry, no need to fuss
In the morning they're the same kids
Boarding the big yellow school bus

America

A land of the brave and free
My home, my birthplace a warm
place to be
Every American should be proud
Ring out bells! Ring them LOUD!

In America you can be whomever
you want to be
There's no place like it on earth
Bountiful, beautiful and blessed
        Seasons of
Winter snow, Spring rains, Summer
sun, Fall's glory
elegantly dressed

Americans are so giving, hard-
working making and sharing their
living
There's a spirit in America second
to none

"Try your best, pass the test be
number one"

From North to South East to West
American has a right to boast from
coast to coast
It embraces all who want to be free
        Come and see
American stands for God's given liberty

Penny Johnson

Everlasting Freedom

If I were given only one wish
Here is what it would be
I would wish everyone in the
whole world would be free
Free to be whatever they wanted
to be! Not license! Free
        Yes! Yes!
That is my wish for you from me
Go now and be what you were meant to be
Always and forever totally free

Fighting For Freedom

There's a special kind of American
Our brave and selfless fighting man
Even in the year nineteen ninety
nine, fighting women put their lives
on the line
For senseless hatred of people who are
being killed needlessly
Our Freedom Fighters refuse to let
it be

Whether on land or sea or sky
To fight for freedom, they will
die for people they don't even know
When they are called, they will go

As they cross over to the other shore
We could never love them more
Fighting for freedom on the other
side, they are our nation's pride

Penny Johnson

A Love Song

My husband, my heart we're
together, but apart When did
she steal you away
Was it midnight or on a sunny
day

Did she wear red satin or black lace
I knew she had you by the look on
your face
She's a robber and a thief and not
at all fair, I could fight her but
how when she's only thin air
She won't win her treacherous game
Alzheimer is her name
She wants you, she wants what I've
got
She'll not have you, she will not
You don't know it my husband, my dear

But I love you still, always did and
always will

(For Judy and Woody who won their race)

"The Wedding"

The Bride was dressed in a veil, white
ivory and lace, the Groom wearing a white coat
dark pants had a smile on his face, She was 18,
he, 21, their life together had just begun
The bride's maids carried French nosegays
and were dressed in pink and blue, the grooms-
men in white and rosebuds were wonderful too
The bride's bouquet, an orchid wrapped around
a white Bible with satin bows and tied in a
lover's knot, candles, music, family and
friends could never be forgot-like Camelot
A shared piece of cake, fruit punch, hugs
and kisses, racing toward the decorated
car showered with rice and best wishes A
beautiful start, solemn vows never to part,
the year 1958-joined-each the other's mate,
still together, still in love year
1999 anniversary 41
Because of the way "The Wedding" had begun
Now the year 2004, married almost 46 years
The joy, happiness, and cheers far out
weigh the sorrow or tears

Penny Johnson

Delight

Somewhere between daylight and midnight
comes twilight, not quite day and not quite night
Then a big black blanket spreads across the
sky "No light" – Next specks of light come
"twinkling" out – "starlight"
One by one they face, "Midnight" Soon rays
of light peek through, they become brilliant
"sunlight"
One day ends, another begins, peaceful morning
light
Pure delight!

A Bouquet of Poets

A Mother's verse and rhyme is about love
everytime, she is a Rose
Nursery school children will tell of
their puppy or cat they are Babies Breath
and that's that
Pre-teens will tell of friendship
and fun
A sunny side of life, their joy has just
begun, they are Buttercups
Teenagers are so colorful, so alive
They are Four O'clocks – they just can't wait
to be five
Grandparents so stately and tall, they are Iris
They stand above all
Now Father, what kind of flower is he
sensitive yet strong, pick a flower for him
It seems kind of silly, but because of every-
thing he is there is one and it can only be a
Tiger-Lily

Outback

In the flower garden so fair, bunches
of flower heads bounced in the air
Pink and purple phlox, pretty daisies
and roses red
Petunias and lilies slept in their beds
Wild flowers of every hue, purple,
violet and cornflower blue
One solitary flower pushed up from the
ground, grew taller and taller than any
around
He was alone, there was no other
No Father or Mother, Sister or Brother
But he grew bigger than any other
There aroma was simply grand
His beauty and glory was just to stand
TALL
When he was through growing, he was bigger
than all
His blossoms were yellow, in his center was
an eye, he turned his face upward toward
the sky
As rain came down, he took a drink
Afterwards he the only "Sunflower" in
the garden gave the sun a "wink"

Small Poems That Say Special Things

Penny Johnson

Hands

Hands that help
Hands that heal
My mother's hands
As a nurse, she is a gift

A Magic Moment

Star-kissed night
Flickering candlelight
Music in the air
Gardenias in my hair
Perfume
and YOU

Penny Johnson

A Special Joy

On Thursday morn, a colt
was born
To everyone's delight
As our gaze met, how his
eyes did shine and the
last thing I thought
when I looked at him
was, I wish that he were mine

Sensational Season

Sunbeams
Umbrellas
Moonlight
Mists
Everything enjoyable
(especially ice cream)
Rainbows, of course
SUMMER

Penny Johnson

Flight of Fantasy

I am free
I can be anything
I want to be
My pencil, my paper,
and me

A Little Bird Told Me

I awoke this morning with a start
To the rapid beating of my own heart
Outside the wind was moaning
Inside the house was groaning
Torrents of rain came tumbling
down
Beating their way into the ground
I looked out the window and saw
A little bird – caught away from
his warm secure nest, he passed
the test, he did his best
Drenched and cold – he shivered
he quivered
But hovering down against the
wind, he dug his claws, in my
window sill
Then rising up from his throat
and out his bill, he started
to sing
A most astonishing thing!
So whatever trouble comes my
way today, I'm gonna keep on
singing anyway

The Symbol

I don't agree with you and
You don't agree with me
Let's go to war!
I'll kill some of you
And you kill some of me
What's left of you will
kill what's left of me
But, we still won't agree

Let's don't go to war
Why?
Because children die
Instead, let's plant a tree
We will name it Tolerance
It will be the great divide
You stay on your and I'll
stay on my side
Remember they tree
Eventually we will learn to
agree to disagree

Comfort From My Grandparents

Chilled, I asked my Grandmother,
"Why did Billy die?"
He was only ten
I wanted to know why!

Pained, I searched her face
What could she say?
"Child," she said gently,
"The old must die and the
young may"

Awed and helpless, I tried
to be brave
"Sweetbaby, life is a struggle
from the cradle to the grave,"

Grandfather said
"But the Lord knows best"
"Twas then that I could let
Billy rest

Majestic Words That Magnify

"I have a Dream Today," Martin Luther King
"Ask not what your country can do for you,
ask what you can do for your country,"
John F. Kennedy
"In spite of everything I still believe
people are good at heart," Ann Frank
"Give me Liberty or Give Me Death,"
Patrick Henry
"I Regret That I Have Only One Life to
Give for my Country," Nathan Hale
"Let's all go Home and Pray for one
another," Robert F. Kennedy
"War is too Horrible for Any Human to
Have to Experience," Dwight David Eisen-
hower
"It IS Finished," Jesus the Christ
Words that stick in our minds like
Blackstrap molasses and cause tears
to flow from beneath our eyelashes

Pride of the Bluegrass

Who's the best band in the land?
We yell "Lexington Lafayette High School
Band"
And what makes it that way? Practice,
practice everyday, left right left right
we march together, guide right eyes bright
no matter what the weather
Learn the notes, hear the sound, take the
field march round and round
Band camp, work hard everyday, but to be
The Champions it's the only way-wear Tee shirts
shorts and tennis shoes, learn marches, classics
and the blues, mentally coming together hand
in hand, first performance in "Sharp" uniforms
we're "the band"
Through football season, contests until the
Christmas parade all of our goals we have made
Watch our red or white plumes atop our hats
We strut like one person in blue uniforms and
white spats
"Grand Champions Class 4 A are we"
How did we do it? Don't you see, we paid the
price we built our band to be the finest in
our land
Our love for each other, music and marching
Made us better than any other

Wildcat's Roar

The University of Kentucky basket-
ball team had a dream
It wanted to be the Nation's Number
one team
Thunder down the floor, make a
basket,
pass and run, miss a basket, screaming
fans join in the fun
Number one Coach, Rick Pitino and his
wife JoAnne believed the Wildcats
could achieve greatness in the zone
or man to man
"Never give up, never give in, stay
in the game until you win"
National Champions 1996-U.K.
Wildcats Roar

The Perfect Name

She had three puppies in her arms, each
was special and had it's own charms, one
was snow white like his mother, Abbie's
face, another was tan with a cute little up-
turned face
The third was strawberry blond with curly
eyelashes
The other two puppies fat tummies barely
left him a space, Cocker Spaniel was their
breed
We did not hesitate, there was no need
The strawberry blond one with the floppy
ears would become ours
He would live for years and years
From day one he was feisty, it was going
to be hard to tame him
He'd learned to sit up and shake paws with
you and his favorite game was to "worry"
a shoe
He was our darling, a most special dog
Our Joy! Looking back it wasn't hard to
name him
He was Abbie's Skippy Boy

The Way To Christianity

Simply say, gentle Jesus, sweet and kind
enter into this heart of mine,

Where you are is where I want to be
To live throughout eternity

      WHY?

Because you first loved me

Wonder of Wonders

They say He walked on water
Walked on water?
With his voice he calmed
the sea
Calmed the sea?
He healed one with leprosy
One who had leprosy?
Changed water to wine
Water to wine?
Fruit of the vine, wine
They say He did so many things
It would fill more than one
book
Fill more than one book?
Now look,
He unstopped a deaf man's ears
He could then hear
He could hear?
He made a man, blind from birth
see
Made him see?

How could it be that they are
right
After thousands of years
Jesus, the Majestic healed me!
Even me?

Answered Prayer

Though I am grown, I am your child
Lord, you said in your word I could
have anything if I asked in your name
I asked for fortune and fame, no answer
came
Down on my knees hour after hour
"Okay, Lord, I demanded, then give me
power"
Still the same, no answer came
But, you gave me warm bread to eat
and honey-sweet
Dear friends and loved ones to greet
Cool, fresh water to drink
A brain with which to reason and think
No need to bargain or plead
I have all I really need
So today I will pray in a different
way
A prayer I know I'll get an answer to
It is, Heavenly Father is there anything
that I can do for you?

I Believe

Jesus loves me
I will love Him
Yes I will, yes I will
I will talk with Him
Yes I will, yes I will
I will walk with Him
Yes I will, yes I will
I will shout with Him
Yes I will, yes I will
I will wait for Him
Yes I will, yes I will
Until He comes for me
Yes He will, yes He will

There Is No Death

Roses are asleep beneath the snow
They'll rise soon, maybe May
Perhaps June

It's painful not to see them
And one day we will be them
For we will need to sleep too
But now we have work to do

When roses rise from their rest
They'll see light, feel warmth
And look their best

Roses will rise from beneath the snow
Because Jesus says so

Heaven Awaits

If I live my life right
Love my neighbors as myself
with all my might
Put God first and foremost
Push away pride try not to boast

When I win first prize for my
blueberry pie
It can't compete with a gorgeous
blue sky
Fill my allotted days to help others
Make people of all nations my
sisters and brothers

Thankfully
I know for sure, without a doubt
In the fullness of time
Heaven awaits me with a SHOUT!

Glory Bound

Lord, when my life is over and my
days on earth are through, I'm not
exactly certain how I'm supposed to
get to You
Don't drop down a ladder from Heaven to
the ground with Angels going up and
Angels coming down or send a fiery
chariot (that's just like you) just send
a simple donkey to ride like Jesus used
to do, I'll climb upon his back, find
his neck and wrap my arms around
He'll know how to use his hoofs and head them
"Glory Bound" As we go up, up through the skies
of blue let those I've left behind me know
I lived my life, trying to get to you
When we reach Heaven's gate open the doors
and we'll crash through, then we'll be where
we belong, with Jesus and with You
Don't send an Host of Angels with Harps of
Gold to set me free
Just a simple donkey
What's good enough for Jesus is good enough
for me

Hope

We all have pain
We all have sorrow
Let's just get through today
And welcome tomorrow

About the Author

Poet Penny Johnson was born in Danville, Kentucky, but she lives in Lexington, Kentucky, heart of the Bluegrass Her mailing address is P.O. Box 8013, Gardenside Branch, Lexington, Kentucky 40504

Penny Johnson was interviewed on the Poetry Today radio show by hostess, Florence Henderson International Star, Television Personality and Singer in New York City with an audience of 16 million listeners on their way into the city to work

Her poem "A Bouquet of Poets" was read. Another poet said that if one poem she wrote made one person happy, she was a success. Penny told Florence she liked that poet and what she said

Penny is an International Poet She is listed in the International Poetry Hall of Fame and Who's Who in Poetry She is a member of The National Author's Registry and can use N.A. following her name She is a semi-finalist in the International Society of Poet's International Poetry Open She holds an Honorary Doctory of Letters from London, England

A member of The American Association of Christian Counselors, she is a Certified Christian Lay Counselor and is happy to help anyone who needs Assistance.

www.ingramcontent.com/pod-product-compliance
Lightning Source LLC
Chambersburg PA
CBHW060356130626
46553CB00003B/1254